Poems on Values to Succeed Worldwide in Life:
Understanding and Wisdom

Simple and Insightful

O.K. FATAI

Published by OK Publishing

Wellington, New Zealand

Copyright © 2019 O.K. Fatai

Email: OK.Publishingnz@gmail.com

Full catalogue information may be obtained from the National Library of New Zealand

All rights reserved.

The moral right of the author has been asserted

ISBN-13: 978-0-9951213-0-0

All rights reserved. No part of this publication may be reproduced, stored in a retrieval system or transmitted in any form by any means electronic, mechanical, photocopying, recording or otherwise, without prior permission from the publisher.

DEDICATION

To all those who strive to understand and grow in understanding.

Contents

It is great	10
We are seekers	11
It is difficult	12
A question	13
Outward and inward	14
Lift it up	15
It is great	16
Outcome	17
Will we?	18
If we look back	19
Transforming	21
Really knowing	22
Went to space	23
Abilities and experiences	24
Door and key	25
Deep connection	26
Goes on	27
Treasures	28
Changing and turning	29
It is like	30

Takes in	31
Other books by O.K. Fatai	32
More books by O.K. Fatai	33
About the Author	35

ACKNOWLEDGMENTS

Family, friends and others who are showing to others in society what it means to live lives that are filled with understanding.

Success Worldwide in Life through Understanding

It is great

It is great to understand nature's law
it is great to understand business principles

it is great to understand the mysteries of history
but it is greater to understand love

it is greater to understand others
and it is greater to understand
what it truly means to be human.

O.K. FATAI

We are seekers

We are seekers of an unknown universe
we are seekers of a mysterious nature

we are seekers of complex galaxies
we are seekers to understand

many unanswered questions of science
as we seek to understand the complexities of life

let's also seek to understand the
life giving gifts of grace and mercy
the living essence of the souls and spirits

POEMS ON VALUES TO SUCCEED WORLDWIDE

It is difficult

Sometimes it is difficult to understand others
sometimes it is difficult to understand your wife

sometimes it is difficult to understand your husband
sometimes it is difficult to understand your children

sometimes it is difficult to understand your friends
sometimes it is difficult to understand your colleagues

sometimes it is difficult to understand your relatives
when it becomes difficult to understand others

try speaking the language of love
for everyone can feel and understand the feelings

of being touched by words and actions of love

O.K. FATAI

A question

There is a question that is often asked
do we understand the questions of physics and chemistry

and do we understand the questions of a child
and do we understand the mysteries of life

and do we understand the complexities of justice
while I do not offer the right answer to these questions

it is worth mentioning that it is equally important
to start with the first thing everyone should understand

which is the understanding of the self
and whether we understand ourselves?

POEMS ON VALUES TO SUCCEED WORLDWIDE

Outward and inward

We like to look at the outward
and understand all there is to know outside us

and through education we learn to know more
about the outward questions that puzzles humans

and while this is important
it is equally important to look inward

and understand all there is to know inside us
the spirit and the soul

eternity and everlasting
grace and mercy
love and forgiveness

for they are the golden principles of life
that we must all seek to fully understand first

O.K. FATAI

Lift it up

Sometimes we don't understand
why this and that happen to us

we don't understand why bad things
happen to people who are really good

we don't understand why bad things
happen to us in our journeys as well

we don't really understand why people
really suffer so much in life

the abused, the discriminated, the oppressed,
the murdered, the persecuted, the refugees,

the children and so much more
life seems to be so unfair

and sometimes hard to understand
and when we meet things that we

don't really understand in life
it is truly great and timely

to lift it up, lift everything up
to the Divine who truly understands.

It is great

It is great to understand things
it is great to achieve high marks in exams

it is a source of much joy and optimism
it is great to know who is doing this

and who is receiving that
it is a great feeling to be able to understand

the different mysteries of life
but sometimes it is also great to accept

who we really are and have the understanding
that sometimes in life it is better to live

the explanation of the mysteries of life
to the Divine who understands us more than
anyone.

Outcome

The outcome of so much understanding
sometimes lead to the belief

that we are beyond others
it leads to the belief

that life is controlled by us and no one else
but when we truly understand life

we will come to truly know
that we are a very small grain of sand

over a vast and a universe that is truly beyond
and when we know that we are but a grain of sand

we will appreciate more the place we have in life
and how truly blessed we are to be part of this
universe

Will we?

As humanity progress
there is a question will we be able

to understand everything there is to know?
will we be able to be a greater part

of this universe and be able to go to
distant and vast galaxies and stars

that are way beyond our own?
our understanding of the mysteries

of the universe is growing each day
and as we seek to understand more

and more of what makes this universe
let us not forget that we must not

loose sight of the Divine
who imparts to us those understandings

O.K. FATAI

If we look back

If we look back to our journeys
over the more than a million years

we can see the progress that we had
gone through over all those years

and if we look back we will learn
lessons that shouldn't be forgotten

lessons about loving peace and
hating violence, lessons about loving

forgiveness and hating oppressions,
lessons about treating every human

with dignity and reverence
but when we look back

we had made so much progress
technologically but not in our treatment

of other human beings
there are still oppression and persecutions

there are still war and unforgiveness
there are still so much pains in life

this may show that we haven't really understand
what it truly means to be human

but there is hope that the Divine will help us
be really us

POEMS ON VALUES TO SUCCEED WORLDWIDE

Success Worldwide in Life through Wisdom

O.K. FATAI

Transforming

The movie is called "*Transformer*"
moving living vehicles

that transformed into different entities
whether it is something that flies

or something that fights with power,
we can transform our lives

even when it is filled with enemies and
mistakes

we can transform our lives
even when they are filled with distress and regrets

for enemies and mistakes
distress and regrets
can truly become a source of wisdom.

Really knowing

We pursue knowledge through learning
we pursue experiences through working

we pursue wellbeing through good food and exercise
really knowing how to live well in society is wisdom

really knowing how to connect with others is wisdom
really knowing how to maintain wellbeing is wisdom

sometimes we know so much without really knowing
sometimes we experience so much without really knowing

wisdom is about really knowing

Went to space

I imagine myself going into deep space
where life cannot really live

deep space filled with darkness
deep space filled with void
deep space filled with silence
deep space filled with nothingness

sometimes wisdom is found in the darkness
sometimes wisdom is found in the void

sometimes wisdom is found in the nothingness
sometimes wisdom is found in the silence of deep space

deep space that can only to be found in the soul and spirits
deep space that can only be found in hearts and minds

Abilities and experiences

Wisdom is not just abilities
it is also about inabilities

wisdom is not just experiences
it is also about inexperiences

it is in our inabilities that we learn new things
it is in our inabilities that we persist

it is in our inabilities that we persevere
it is in our inabilities that we try to understand

it is in our inexperience that we try to experience
it is in our inexperience that we try to progress

so do value your abilities and inabilities
and value your experiences and inexperiences
for they are all sources of wisdom.

O.K. FATAI

Door and key

The door to the castle of wisdom
is often called experience

the key to the door of the castle is often called
curiosity

sometimes that is not the case
for the door is build and owned by the Divine

and the key to the door is made and owned by the
Divine
and real wisdom comes from the Divine.

Deep connection

It is by deep connection with
nature, others and ourselves
that we get wisdom

it is by deep connection with our
past, our present and our future
that we find wisdom

it is by deep connection with our
mistakes, errors and shortfalls
that we get wisdom

it is by deep connection with our
experiences and inexperiences
that we find wisdom

it is by deep connection with God
and the Divine that we find wisdom
so do practice and live a deep connected life

O.K. FATAI

Goes on

Marvel the knowledge gained
from schooling

while you can
for schooling is learning gained
for a limited time

wisdom is an endeavour
that goes on in perpetuity

it's more than lifelong
it is eternal

Treasures

Even the stones of gold
and rubies and uncut diamonds

the promises of financial security
and becoming a multi-millionaire

while they are all good things to have
they do not measure up to the

value that wisdom brings to
a person's life

for wisdom is something that cannot
be valued, it is above value.

O.K. FATAI

Changing and turning

Sometimes wisdom is about changing,
changing the way we do things

changing from being self-opinionated
to other opinionated

changing from being a self-promoter
to other promoter

changing from being self-centred
to other centred

and changing the mistakes
we had gone through

into opportunities to
learn and gain wisdom.

It is like

Wisdom is like a lighthouse
that can show us the safe
way to go

wisdom is like a vessel
that can take us to our desired
destination

wisdom in like a safe harbour
that can shelter us from the storms of life
wisdom is like a rock

that we can use as a foundation
for a house to build on
wisdom is a seed that can

grow and bear many enjoyable fruits
wisdom is like a plus sign
it is something that
add positive things to our lives.

O.K. FATAI

Takes in

Wisdom takes in
but never explodes

it is calm in angry times
it is in consideration in tough times
it is reaching out in bad times

it is taking in and not lashing out
it is thoughtful deliberation before speaking
it is something that we all admire and desire to have
every single day of our lives.

Other books by O.K. Fatai

1. Poems on Values to Succeed Worldwide in Life: Being Responsible
2. Poems on Values to Succeed Worldwide in Life: Courage
3. Poems on Values to Succeed Worldwide in Life: Good Families
4. Poems on Values to Succeed Worldwide in Life: Forgiveness
5. Poems on Values to Succeed Worldwide in Life: Good Friends
6. Poems on Values to Succeed Worldwide in Life: Grace
7. Poems on Values to Succeed Worldwide in Life: Hope
8. Poems on Values to Succeed Worldwide in Life: Humility
9. Poems on Values to Succeed Worldwide in Life: Joy
10. Poems on Values to Succeed Worldwide in Life: Justice
11. Poems on Values to Succeed Worldwide in Life: Life
12. Poems on Values to Succeed Worldwide in Life: Love
13. Poems on Values to Succeed Worldwide in Life: Mercy
14. Poems on Values to Succeed Worldwide in Life: Peace
15. Poems on Values to Succeed Worldwide in Life: Perseverance
16. Poems on Values to Succeed Worldwide in Life: Faith
17. Poems on Values to Succeed Worldwide in Life: Harmony

with Nature

18. Poems on Values to Succeed Worldwide in Life: Education

More books by O.K. Fatai

1. Poems on Values to Succeed Worldwide in Life: Understanding and Wisdom

2. Poems on Values to Succeed Worldwide in Life: Work and Optimism

3. Poems on Values to Succeed Worldwide in Life: Adversity and Confidence

4. Poems on Values to Succeed Worldwide in Life: Listening and Diversity and Unity

5. Poems on Values to Succeed Worldwide in Life: Sharing and Honesty

6. Poems on Values to Succeed Worldwide in Life: Simplicity and Harmony

7. Poems on Values to Succeed Worldwide in Life: Unity in Diversity and Connections

8. Poems on Values to Succeed Worldwide in Life: Contentment and Acceptance

9. Poems on Values to Succeed Worldwide in Life: Excellence and Compassion

10. Poems on Values to Succeed Worldwide in Life: Generosity and Being Passionate

11. Poems on Values to Succeed Worldwide in Life: Gentleness and Trustworthy

POEMS ON VALUES TO SUCCEED WORLDWIDE

12. Poems on Values to Succeed Worldwide in Life: Patience and Being Tactful

13. Poems on Values to Succeed Worldwide in Life: Purity and Integrity

14. Poems on Values to Succeed Worldwide in Life: Being Modest and Persistence

15. Poems on Values to Succeed Worldwide in Life: Respect and Loyalty

16. Poems on Values to Succeed Worldwide in Life: Self-Discipline and Orderliness

17. Poems on Values to Succeed Worldwide in Life: Service and Going the Extra Mile

18. Poems on Values to Succeed Worldwide in Life: Sincerity and Honour

19. Poems on Values to Succeed Worldwide in Life: Nature and Reliability

20. Poems on Values to Succeed Worldwide in Life: Helpfulness and Consideration

21. Poems on Values to Succeed Worldwide in Life: Preparedness and Visionary

22. Poems on Values to Succeed Worldwide in Life: Reverence and Thankfulness

23. Poems on Values to Succeed Worldwide in Life: Wonders and Cooperation

O.K. FATAI

About the Author

O.K. Fatai is a poet and author from Wellington, New Zealand. He likes to spend time writing poems, especially ones that explore the different aspects of values and virtues that are widely accepted in different cultures today.

O.K. Fatai also likes to write songs and some of his forthcoming books are song lyrics that also look at different values and virtues and some of their appeal to us today. In his spare time, he writes short stories and novels. He is looking forward to sharing these stories with readers around the world, and he has already published some short stories and has more than ten forthcoming publications in children's literature. O.K. Fatai is also writing novels for young adults and adults. He is also a playwright and has written and/or directed more than eight short plays.

He likes painting abstract art and enjoys the different interpretations of abstract paintings, especially when they reflect values and virtues. He is also a photographer who likes to take photographs of nature and the environment, which has a special place in his heart. He is keen on filming and editing videos as well, plays musical instruments and is part of a local band.

O.K. Fatai is a volunteer at the United Nations and regional prisons in Wellington and, for many years, had volunteered to more than ten other organizations. He works in the health sector and is also a consultant for three different online companies, and the President and CEO of more than three businesses. He is also available as an external consultant to the United Nations, the European Bank for Reconstruction and Development, and the Asian Development Bank.

POEMS ON VALUES TO SUCCEED WORLDWIDE

O.K. FATAI

POEMS ON VALUES TO SUCCEED WORLDWIDE

O.K. FATAI

POEMS ON VALUES TO SUCCEED WORLDWIDE

www.ingramcontent.com/pod-product-compliance
Lightning Source LLC
Chambersburg PA
CBHW020432010526
44118CB00010B/536